www.osha.gov

I0464574

Occupational Safety and Health Act of 1970
"To assure safe and healthful working conditions for working men and women; by authorizing enforcement of the standards developed under the Act; by assisting and encouraging the States in their efforts to assure safe and healthful working conditions; by providing for research, information, education, and training in the field of occupational safety and health..."

This publication provides a general overview of worker rights under the *Occupational Safety and Health Act* (OSH Act). This publication does not alter or determine compliance responsibilities which are set forth in OSHA standards and the OSH Act. Moreover, because interpretations and enforcement policy may change over time, for additional guidance on OSHA compliance requirements the reader should consult current administrative interpretations and decisions by the Occupational Safety and Health Review Commission and the courts.

This information will be made available to sensory-impaired individuals upon request. Voice phone: (202) 693-1999; teletypewriter (TTY) number: 1-877-889-5627.

Hydraulic Fracturing and Flowback Hazards Other than Respirable Silica

U.S. Department of Labor
Occupational Safety and Health Administration

OSHA 3763-12 2014

U.S. Department of Labor

Disclaimer

This guidance document is not a standard or regulation and it creates no new legal obligations. The document is advisory in nature, informational in content, and is intended to assist employers in providing a safe and healthful workplace. The *Occupational Safety and Health Act* requires employers to comply with safety and health standards promulgated by OSHA or by a state with an OSHA-approved state plan. In addition, the Act's Section 5(a)(1), the General Duty Clause, requires employers to provide their workers with a workplace free from recognized hazards likely to cause death or serious physical harm. Employers can be cited for violating the General Duty Clause if there is a recognized hazard and they do not take reasonable steps to prevent or abate the hazard. However, failure to implement any specific recommendations contained within this document is not, in itself, a violation of the General Duty Clause. Citations can only be based on standards, regulations, and the General Duty Clause.

Table of Contents

This publication informs employers and workers about the known hazards that result from hydraulic fracturing and flowback and identifies ways to reduce exposure to these hazards. It does not include a detailed discussion of the silica hazards workers potentially experience during hydraulic fracturing operations. For more information on those hazards, refer to the OSHA and NIOSH Hazard Alert entitled, "Worker Exposure to Silica during Hydraulic Fracturing" and the OSHA Infosheet, "Silica Exposure during Hydraulic Fracturing". When addressing the hazards associated with these operations, in addition to this document, employers must follow applicable OSHA regulations and consult specific company guidelines. Also, before beginning work, personnel should receive instruction in hazard recognition and safe work practices to reduce the chance of injury on the job site.

Introduction

Hydraulic fracturing is a treatment process that stimulates well production in the upstream oil and gas industry. While not a new process, hydraulic fracturing has been increasingly used in the last ten years due to the increase in horizontal well development, which requires multiple stimulation stages per well. Hydraulic fracturing involves pumping large volumes of fluid blended with proppant and chemicals at pressures necessary to fracture a hydrocarbon-containing formation. Once the fractures are created, proppants are placed within the fractures to hold them open and allow for the release and flowback of fluids and hydrocarbons. For an overview of typical hydraulic fracturing and flowback operations, see the simplified flow sheet in Appendix A, *Flow Chart of Processes.*

Each year, an estimated 35,000 wells are hydraulically-fractured in the U.S.[1] Although the oil and gas extraction industry as a whole has a relatively higher fatality rate compared to most of the U.S. general industry (see Appendix B), there is currently no worker injury/illness or fatality data publicly available for hydraulic fracturing or flowback operations. Regardless of the availability of data, more workers are potentially exposed to the hazards created by hydraulic fracturing and flowback operations due to the large increase in the number of these operations in the past decade. In light of this, OSHA has determined that additional information concerning hydraulic fracturing and flowback operations hazards should be provided to educate and protect workers.

---

[1] American Petroleum Institute (API) HF2, Water Management Associated with Hydraulic Fracturing, 2010.

The table of contents lists primary tasks associated with hydraulic fracturing and flowback, the detailed hazard information, and suggestions for mitigation follow in the body of the document.

Pre-Job Planning and Safety Meeting

- Each hydraulic fracturing job should be thoroughly planned and its hazards identified.

- Prior to the work beginning and at each shift change, all personnel on site should participate in a pre-job safety meeting appropriate for the level of risk to discuss the job's upcoming tasks, responsibilities, hazards, and mitigation.

- Each work team should participate in a discussion that may include procedures, pre-job checklists, safe work permits, simultaneous operations, and emergency response procedures.

- Additional meetings should be held throughout the day if the scope of work or personnel changes significantly.

- Workers should be encouraged to exercise a 'Stop work authority' for unsafe conditions or practices.

- All incidents and injuries should be reported immediately.

- Ensure that workers only undertake work for which they are trained to carry out and/or under appropriate supervision.

Appendix C – *Links to Additional Resources*, provides links to supplemental information related to sections of this guidance document. A matrix is included in Appendix D – *Potential Hazards Related to the Job Steps of Hydraulic Fracturing* detailing many of the job steps and the associated hazards.

Before work begins workers gather for a pre-job meeting.

Section I – Hazards during Transport, Rig-Up, and Rig-Down

Serious injuries and fatalities have resulted from worker exposure to both off-site and on-site vehicle and machinery traffic or movement. Incidents have occurred when workers travel to and from well sites on highways and other roadways. Further, workers have been killed and injured at well sites where moving vehicles and equipment have created hazards to workers.

Prevention Strategies: Transportation

Vehicle traffic at the worksite can present a significant hazard before, during, and after hydraulic fracturing. Additionally, more workers are on site during these operations and many of these sites can be small and congested, increasing the risk to workers. Steps can be taken to reduce worker exposure to the hazards related to multiple vehicles and machines (including water, sand, chemical, iron, mixing equipment, pumping, and other rigs) that are driven through or pulled into position on these sites.

Congested area due to a large amount of equipment and confined work area.

Some additional publications related to vehicle hazards are listed in Appendix C.

Employers can take the following precautions to prevent transportation-related incidents, both on the road and at or near well sites:

- Emphasize to drivers and workers the need to stay alert and follow the established rules for vehicle traffic safety. This includes both travel to the well site (journey management) as well as vehicle and equipment movement at or near the well pad.

- Establish and implement an action plan to protect workers during rig-up and rig-down. Raise awareness among workers of their role in this plan during the pre-job safety meeting or similar meetings conducted prior to the start of work, including knowledge and understanding of the worksite staging, unloading, and equipment/vehicle siting locations before beginning these operations.

- Develop and implement on-site work rules related to wearing brightly-colored or reflective vests, which increase worker visibility in areas of vehicle movement.

- Inform workers of the location of public and private access roads, power lines, obstacles, vehicle traffic hazards, controls, and speed limits.

- Remind workers that heavy loads may be harder to stop, and that top-heavy loads may require slower turning and wider turning areas.

- Establish a plan and review rules regarding when spotters are needed/required (e.g., backing up large equipment, vehicles, and operating cranes).

- Allow only essential personnel, i.e., spotters, to be in close proximity to equipment during the backing up of that equipment.

- Encourage workers to request additional lighting where needed. Verify that any lighting spotted in Class 1, Division 1 or 2 areas is approved for the location. *See* 29 CFR 1910.307 – Hazardous (Classified) Locations for mandatory requirements.

- Clearly mark, barricade, or otherwise section off wellhead equipment and guy wires to avoid collision with moving trucks.

Prevention Strategies: Hydraulic Fracturing Rig-Up and Rig-Down Mechanical and Manual Handling

Workers are exposed to heavy equipment, mechanical material handling, manual lifting, and ergonomic hazards during rig-up and rig-down. Rig-up is an oil and gas term that refers to the on-site delivery, construction and connection of components (iron). Rig-down is the term related to the dismantling and removal of the equipment. A number of actions can be taken to prevent injuries (e.g., struck-by, caught-in, and crushing hazards, and musculoskeletal injuries) and fatalities due to the size and weight of the equipment being brought in, unloaded, staged, and assembled.

The potential hazards of moving and handling large, heavy loads can be controlled when employers develop and implement safe work procedures and practices. Employers can take the following precautions to prevent incidents during these types of operations:

- Perform all rig-up and rig-down activities according to the pre-plan and under appropriate supervision.

- Verify the ground is well compacted and level prior to lifting and staging equipment and loads. After severe weather events (e.g., high winds, heavy rain, flooding, etc.) inspect and verify that ground stability has not been adversely affected.

- Allow only trained and qualified operators to operate mobile lifting and hoisting equipment. *See* 29 CFR 1910.178 – Powered Industrial Trucks and 29 CFR 1910.180 – Crawler, Locomotive, and Truck Cranes for mandatory requirements.

- Conduct a hazard assessment at each site, which evaluates hazards associated with handling large, heavy loads.

- Examine equipment to see if it is properly stabilized, anchored, and flagged or marked as necessary for visibility.

- Determine whether sufficient space exists between equipment and materials and that workers stay clear so they are less likely to be crushed by unexpected movement of equipment and/or material.

- Establish a lifting safe zone. Equipment operators and other lift team personnel need to be instructed to never lift suspended loads over workers. *See* 29 CFR 1910.184(c)(9) – Slings for mandatory requirements.

- Instruct workers at the well site to stand clear of suspended loads.

- Train workers to stand clear before the load is unsecured from its transport and during its removal from transport equipment.

- Instruct and verify that loads are only lifted over wells during installation of well control or intervention equipment.

- Instruct workers utilizing tag lines, e.g., spotters, to keep and maintain an adequate distance from the drop zone in case the load is dropped or tumbled. Use a sufficient number of tag lines to ensure stability.

- Workers on foot should have a clear path planned for escape in the event of a dropped or out-of-control load and they should never walk backwards.

- Train workers in proper lifting mechanics when they are required to manually lift loads and to seek assistance when lifting heavy objects.

Prevention Strategies: Rig-Up and Rig-Down General Hazards

Employers can take these additional steps during rig-up and rig-down to prevent worker injury during these operations:

- Erect and maintain wind direction indicators to assure safe egress.

- Identify and maintain emergency egress paths and communicate the emergency plan and pre-designated muster areas to all site personnel.

- Test monitoring, safety equipment and alarms for proper operation.

- Protect workers from falls, as falls from heights and falls at the same level are significant hazards. *See* 29 CFR 1910 Subpart D – Walking-Working Surfaces for mandatory requirements.

- Verify that walking and working surfaces are clear and maintained to reduce the risk of slips, trips and falls.

- Instruct workers to avoid stepping backwards.

- Identify and alert workers to confined spaces, e.g., well cellars, waste water pits and storage tanks or trailers, and their associated hazards at the well site. *See* 29 CFR 1910.146 – Permit-Required Confined Spaces for mandatory requirements.

- Provide engineering controls when technically and economically feasible to reduce noise levels to workers generated by engines, pumps and other equipment, which meet or exceed a 90 dBA, for an 8-hour time-weighted average (TWA). Where worker exposure to noise is at or above an 85 dBA 8-hour TWA, implement a hearing conservation program. Examples of engineering and work practice controls include sound dampers, distancing employees from noise sources and hearing protection. *See* 29 CFR 1910.95 – Occupational Noise Exposure for mandatory requirements.

- Inspect and repair equipment if leaks or other damage is identified before continuing the process. Leaks may occur due to loose hammer unions and other connections, equipment wear and damage. Workers should never hammer on pressurized lines.

- Match hammer union connections with the same pressure rating and thread type. Mismatched hammer unions may fit together, but they can fail suddenly at lower pressures than the rated working pressure of the equipment. Confirmation with a 'go-no go' gauge is recommended.

- Be aware of hammering up iron in extreme cold conditions, e.g., -40 degrees Fahrenheit, as freezing temperatures can lower the impact strength of ferrous materials.

- Develop and implement a hazardous energy or energy-isolation program to control hazards during the servicing or maintenance of equipment and machines.

Such hazards would result from equipment related to hydraulic fracturing, flowback, and other well-completion or well-servicing operations that is being serviced or maintained that releases hazardous energy (e.g., mechanical, hydraulic, pneumatic, chemical, thermal, or other energy) where the energy is not properly controlled.[2]

- Consider using air movers or other equipment and respirators in situations where diesel exhaust at high concentrations may increase the risk of health effects (e.g., eye and nose irritation, headaches and nausea, respiratory disease and lung cancer). *See* OSHA's Safety and Health Topics Page – Diesel Exhaust, for more information.

- Identify and train workers in ergonomic hazards during rig-up and rig-down operations. Appendix C contains more information on ergonomic hazards.

- Monitor weather conditions and weather alerts (e.g., lightening, tornados, high winds, rain and snow).

- Communicate hazards associated with animals, insects, snakes, and plants that could pose a danger to workers.

- Ensure adequate lighting to perform tasks. Verify that any lighting located in Class 1, Division 1 or 2 areas is approved for the location. *See* 29 CFR 1910.307 – Hazardous (Classified) Locations for mandatory requirements.

---

[2] While these operations are exempt from OSHA's 29 CFR 1910.147 – The Control of Hazardous Energy (Lockout/Tagout) standard, this standard could be used by employers to provide safe work practices for the control of hazardous energy. For equipment maintenance and servicing related to electrical hazards, employers must comply with Subpart S – Electrical standard, including 29 CFR 1910.333 – Electrical: Selection and Use of Work Practices. Additionally, employers can consult API's safe work guidelines for the control of hazardous energy (API RP 54, R2007, Section 6.9 – Lockout/Tagout).

Perforating Guns

Employers can take the following precautions with respect to perforating guns:

- Allow only workers trained in perforating operations to handle perforating guns.

- Keep personnel not directly involved clear of the area when loading, unloading or running perforating guns into and out of the wellbore.

- Consult the procedures outlined under American Petroleum Industry (API) RP 67, *Recommended Practice for Oilfield Explosives Safety* (proper grounding, radio transmission signs, proper arming/disarming procedures, etc.) for safe operations of perforating guns.[3]

- Always assume that a gun is live when retrieving it from the wellbore.

- Be sure that after spent guns are retrieved from the wellbore all explosives have detonated and perforation holes are in every port on the gun. This practice will ensure that no unexploded charges are in the gun tube during transport and disposal of perforating guns with scrap dealers.

- Assume guns are pressurized when dismantling. Perforating guns may become pressurized down hole and retain pressure to the surface.

---

[3] API RP 67, Recommended Practice for Oilfield Explosives Safety is offered as a free download from www.api.org.

■ After setting any type of downhole plug/packer with setting tools that utilize an igniter and powder charge, be sure on retrieval that the tools are bled properly of all internal pressure and maintain a safe distance from all personnel when bleeding.

Section II – Hazards during Mixing and Injection

Chemicals used during hydraulic fracturing are significantly diluted with fluid (typically water) and proppant. However to avoid chemical exposure from presenting a potential hazard to workers during unloading, mixing, and blending a number of steps can be taken by employers. To aid employers in identifying effective prevention strategies, the table below lists the potential effects associated with exposure to some of the chemicals that may be used in hydraulic fracturing operations:

Frequently Used Hydraulic Fracturing Chemicals		
Product Function	Chemicals Used	Potential Hazards from Exposure to Chemicals
Proppant	Sand, Manufactured products-ceramics, sintered bauxite	Silicosis (sand), Mechanical irritation of eyes, skin, nose and throat
Acids	Hydrochloric acid, Hydrofluoric acid	Corrosive, irritant to skin, eyes lungs
pH Adjustment	Acids, Bases	Chemical burns, corrosive, irritant to skin, eyes and lungs
Biocides	Aldehydes, Quaternary ammonia compounds	Toxic by direct contact or inhalation. May cause irritation or allergic reactions

Frequently Used Hydraulic Fracturing Chemicals		
Product Function	Chemicals Used	Potential Hazards from Exposure to Chemicals
Friction Reducers	Petroleum distillates, Methanol, Ethylene glycol	Flammable. Some hydrocarbons are suspected carcinogens. May be toxic by ingestion
Gelling agents, Polymers	Guar gum, Polysaccharides, Polyacrylamides	May cause irritation by direct contact or inhalation
Cross Linkers	Sodium tetraborate and other borate salts, Ziconium complexes	Toxic by direct contact or inhalation
Breakers	Magnesium peroxide, Calcium peroxide, Magnesium oxide, Ammonium persulfate	May cause irritation by direct contact, ingestion or inhalation. Peroxides are oxidizers, that may cause a fire or release oxygen that intensifies a fire
Iron Control Agents	Citric acid, Acetic acid, Thioglycolic acid	Corrosive, irritant to skin, eyes and lungs
Scale Inhibitor	Copolymer of Acrylamide and Sodium Acrylate, Sodium polycarboxylate, Phosphonic acid, Salt	Irritant to skin, eyes and lungs
Clay Stabilizers	Choline chloride, Tetramethyl ammonium chloride, Sodium chloride	Hazardous to eyes, skin, lungs and by ingestion
Corrosion Control	Formic Acid, Acetaldehyde	Irritant to skin, eyes and lungs
Surfactants	Lauryl sulfate, alcohols, 2-butoxyethanol	May cause irritation by direct contact, ingestion or inhalation

Source: OSHA's Oil and Gas Well Drilling and Servicing eTool. For more information, see each chemical's Safety Data Sheet or visit: fracfocus.org/chemical-use/what-chemicals-are-used.

Prevention Strategies: Chemical Handling

To minimize exposures during chemical handling, employers can do the following:

- Verify that hazards are identified, properly assessed, and controlled through engineering controls and administrative controls as appropriate.

- Make Safety Data Sheets ("SDS") available to workers who may be handling and/or are exposed to the chemicals. *See* 29 CFR 1910.1200(g), Hazard Communication, Safety Data Sheets for mandatory requirements.

- Make personal protective equipment (PPE) available and use PPE as per a PPE Hazard Assessment. *See* 29 CFR Subpart I – Personal Protective Equipment for mandatory requirements.

- Utilize signage and/or barricades limiting access to essential personnel. Signage should include PPE requirements. *See* 29 CFR 1910.145 – Specifications for Accident Prevention Signs and Tags for mandatory requirements.

- Reduce worker exposure to harmful substances below the permissible exposure limit (PEL) where air sampling indicates levels above OSHA's PELs for a substance. *See* 29 CFR 1910 Subpart Z – Toxic and Hazardous Substances for mandatory requirements.

- "Communicate" the site's Hazard Communication Program ("HazCom") to workers, which would include proper labeling of containers, availability of SDSs and training of employees on the hazardous chemicals in their work area. *See* 29 CFR 1910.1200 – Hazard Communication, for mandatory requirements.

- Train workers on how to respond, including their roles and level of response, to potential chemical spills or leaks when they are involved with the site's Hazardous Waste & Emergency Response ("HAZWOPER") program. *See* 29 CFR 1910.120(q), Emergency Response Program to Hazardous Substance Releases, for mandatory requirements.

- Provide facilities (i.e., safety shower and eyewash stations) for quickly drenching or flushing the eyes and body where workers, eyes or body could be exposed to corrosive materials. Routinely inspect and function test safety showers and eyewash stations. *See* 29 CFR 1910.151(c), Medical Services and First Aid, for mandatory requirements.

- Verify that workers are trained and understand emergency response procedures and the location of safety shower or eyewash stations, escape route, muster point(s), and incident notification and management processes.

- Develop and implement company procedures to safely check chemical containers and transfer lines regularly, verifying there are no leaks.

- Instruct workers to exercise proper personal hygiene, such as washing with soap and water before going onto other activities, when they have contact with chemicals and/or fracturing fluids. Also, train workers to inform their supervisor or medical personnel if symptoms appear.

Note: Exposure to respirable crystalline silica dust poses a significant potential hazard to workers exposed during the unloading, transferring and blending of proppants. As noted earlier in this publication, this hazard is discussed in a separate OSHA/NIOSH Hazard Alert.

Section III – Hazards during Pressure Pumping

In order to minimize potential work hazards from high pressure resulting from uncontrolled releases employers can use a number of prevention strategies.

Prevention Strategies: Pressure Pumping

To reduce the risk of hazards associated with pumping under pressure, employers can use the following prevention practices:

- Develop and implement an effective operating plan and procedure, which include information about the equipment, operating limits, energy isolation, startup and shutdown procedures, normal operations and emergency procedures.

- Develop and implement a communication plan, which includes testing communication devices.

- Set pressure relief devices to discharge at a pressure equal to or less than the rated working pressure of the weakest component (pump, piping, hose, or fitting, etc.) of the system that the devices protect.

- Ensure that workers know and follow the procedures for pressure monitoring during the pumping process.

- Verify the workers' knowledge of the operating limits of their equipment.

- Inspect high pressure lines from the pump trucks to the wellhead before the job begins.

- Walk down equipment on the site using the written procedure as a checklist, and whenever possible, verify valve positions, and relief settings prior to starting work.

- Secure pressure relief device discharge lines or vents and high pressure lines.

- Follow the company's exclusion zone requirements, which allow only essential workers within the specified zone.

- Pressure test the pump and discharge lines at a pressure no less than the maximum expected treating pressure specified, but not to exceed the rated working pressure of the component with the lowest rated working pressure.

- Do not allow anyone to strike a pressurized line or any of their connections. Positively confirm that lines are not pressurized prior to attempting to tighten or loosen hammer unions. Serious injuries and fatalities have resulted.

- Inspect equipment at rig-down, document its condition, and remove suspected defective equipment from service.

Prevention Strategies: Flammable Fluids, Atmospheres, and Materials

Employers can use the following strategies to prevent incidents involving flammable material hazards during operations:

- Remove from the area or shut down (shut off) potential ignition sources including electrical equipment and equipment with internal combustion engines not used in the performance of the job.

- Require workers to wear company-provided flame-resistant clothing if they could be exposed to flash fire hazards. *See* 29 CFR 1910.132 – Personal Protective Equipment, General Requirements, for mandatory requirements.

- Ground and bond all blending equipment to all other equipment used to unload sand into a hopper.

- Communicate to workers that flammable gases may be present as the formations are fractured.

- Monitor the atmosphere for the presence of flammable gases at their lower explosive limit (LEL).

- Erection of a flare during flowback may be necessary to make sure that off gases are safely burned.

- Perform hazard assessments and take precautions if hot-fueling is required. Refueling equipment while engines are running (hot-fueling) poses very serious hazards and consequences.[4]

Note: Internal combustion engines present ignition hazards when used in the presence of flammable vapors or gasses. For additional information, see the OSHA Fact Sheet, *Internal Combustion Engines as Ignition Sources:* www.osha.gov/Publications/osha3589.pdf

Section IV – Hazards during Flowback Operations

Workers in flowback operations need to be aware of potential hazards. Fluid and materials flowing back at very high pressures from the well may contain debris such as rocks and mud, plugs and other parts, methane gas, hydrogen sulfide, oil, water, sand, and small amounts of chemicals

---

[4] See NFPA 385, *Standard for Tank Vehicles for Flammable and Combustible Liquids* and API RP 54, Section 8.2, Fuel and Oil Transfers and Refueling, for additional guidance on safe work practices that apply to these types of fueling operations.

injected into the well during hydraulic fracturing. A number of prevention strategies can be used to minimize piping separation at connection points, leaks, and equipment failures at these pressures, and avoid high-energy uncontrolled events including injuries and fatalities to workers. Many of the pressure controls discussed above for flammable atmosphere and materials also apply to flowback operations.

Photo: Universal Well Services

Flowback setup.

Prevention Strategies: Pressure during Flowback Operations

To prevent pressure-related hazards during flowback, employers can use the following controls:

- Discuss and verify worker understanding of the potential hazards caused from flammable liquids, compressed gases, and high pressures which can result in fires, explosions and/or high-energy releases.

- Restrain or secure high pressure lines including relief lines with proven restraint devices and methods to prevent potential "whipping" of these lines should there be an equipment failure. Unrestrained lines have been known to swing freely, striking workers and equipment.

- ▨ Inspect and test iron and other equipment prior to use. Be aware of possible sand erosion.

- ▨ Maintain and monitor choke manifolds during the flowback operation to ensure that they continue to work properly. These manifolds are a means to reduce the pressure and flow velocity from the well in a controlled manner.

Photo: National STEPS Network

Photo: Universal Well Services

Flowback pipe restraint systems and blocks.

Prevention Strategies: Potential Flammable Atmospheres

Flammable atmospheres are a significant hazard during flowback. Leaks and other uncontrolled releases need only an ignition source once the airborne concentration reaches the lower explosive limit (LEL). Discharge to flowback tanks, tanker trucks, sand separators, oil and gas separators, pits, flares, and other locations may also contain high levels of flammable liquids or gases and may have flammable concentrations in and around them. Areas around tanks or leaks can quickly reach the LEL. An ignition source can be a cigarette, an engine, static charge, cell phone, radio, or other devices.

To control fire and explosion hazards during flowback operations employers can use the following strategies:

■ Inform workers that gas leaks can be difficult to identify because produced gas is colorless and can be odorless.

■ Communicate operating procedures for flowback operations to potentially affected workers.

■ Provide workers with information about the equipment used and safe operating practices for the equipment, startup and shutdown procedures, normal operations, and emergency procedures including site alarms. Train workers in all these procedures and verify their understanding.

■ Establish and implement bonding and grounding procedures as appropriate.

■ Utilize personal and fixed LEL monitors. Routinely test and maintain these devices.

■ Require workers to wear company-provided flame-resistant clothing if they could be exposed to flash fire hazards. Use of a PPE Hazard Assessment can assist employers in identifying worker exposure to this hazard. *See* 29 CFR 1910 Subpart I – Personal Protective Equipment, for mandatory requirements.

- Ensure that safety valves[5] and flares[6] are properly sized and utilized.

- Provide, maintain, and train workers on the use of on-site fire extinguishing equipment. *See* 29 CFR 1910.157 – Portable Fire Extinguishers for mandatory requirements.

- Quickly identify and repair leaks found during the operation as per manufacturer's recommendation or operational guidelines, isolating energy sources and equipment as required.

- Do not allow welding and other activities that will produce heat or ignition sources. If required, perform hot work outside of the flowback areas and authorization (e.g., hot work permit) must be granted prior to the work. *See* 29 CFR Subpart Q, Welding, Cutting, and Brazing, and in particular 29 CFR 1910.252, General Requirements, for standards containing mandatory requirements related to these type of activities.

- Consult applicable guidance information contained in National Fire Protection Association (NFPA) documents, including NFPA 30.[7]

---

[5] For additional guidance, see API RP 54, Recommended Practices for Occupational Safety for Oil and Gas Well Drilling and Servicing Operations, Section 9.13.6, R2007.

[6] For additional guidance, see ANSI/API STANDARD 521, Pressure-relieving and Depressuring Systems, 5th Ed., January 2007.

[7] For additional guidance, see National Fire Protection Association (NFPA) 30, Flammable and Combustible Liquids Code, 2012, as well as other NFPA standards.

Section V – Hydrogen Sulfide (H₂S) and Volatile Organic Compounds (VOCs)

Prevention Strategies: H₂S and VOCs

Some wells may contain elevated levels of H_2S. To protect workers from H_2S exposure, employers may use the following strategies:

- Inform workers that flowback fluids may contain potentially hazardous chemical residues and dissolved solids of minerals in the formation.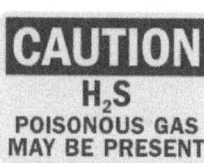

- Instruct workers that they should not depend on their sense of smell for H_2S detection.

- Identify and evaluate the work environment for potential exposures to H_2S for both health and safety reasons. *See* 29 CFR 1910.134(d)(iii) – Respiratory Protection, General Requirements for mandatory requirements.

- Provide appropriate PPE as per the PPE Hazard Assessment to avoid exposure from contaminants. *See* 29 CFR Subpart I – Personal Protective Equipment for mandatory requirements.

- Understand and maintain awareness of wind direction for activity and egress planning. Utilize personal and fixed H_2S monitors. Routinely test and maintain these devices.

- Exit the area quickly when the monitor alarms or where there is other evidence of H_2S.

- Follow the company's procedures for evacuating the site and for reporting and investigating incidents.

- Ensure that workers wash and change clothing if contaminated by process fluids before beginning other activities. Additionally, instruct workers to inform their supervisor or medical personnel of any symptoms that may appear.

Additional OSHA and industry reference standards include OSHA standard 29 CFR 1910.1000, Air contaminants, and API RP 49, *Recommended Practice for Drilling and Well Servicing Operations Involving Hydrogen Sulfide.*

Volatile Organic Compounds (VOCs) and Benzene, Toluene, Ethylbenzene and Xylenes (BTEX)

Some processes and activities can lead to potential VOC exposures (e.g., including BTEX, other aliphatic and aromatic compounds in flowback, and other produced fluids, and mixtures of fuels) that may exceed occupational exposure limits (both STEL and PEL). Benzene, because of its carcinogenic potential, is a chemical of major concern that may also cause short-term toxicity to the nervous system, liver, and kidneys at high concentrations[8]. Other VOCs associated with hydrocarbon production may have the potential to injure organ systems when uncontrolled exposures occur. Inhalation is the primary route of exposure to VOCs. However, they may also enter the body through the skin (dermal) or by mouth (ingestion). Toxicity hazards from many of the VOCs encountered during flowback may

---

[8] ToxFAQs™ for Benzene; Agency for Toxic Substances and Disease Registry; 2007.

occur at airborne concentrations far below their flammability hazard and may present a need for special monitoring to assess the respirable hazard. See the table below for established occupational exposure limits for VOCs. Employers must identify and evaluate respiratory hazards at their worksites. *See* 29 CFR 1910.134(d)(1)(iii), for mandatory requirements.

Occupational Exposure and Flammability Limits for Volatile Organic Compounds

Compound	PEL*	IDLH*	LEL**	UEL**
Benzene	10 ppm	500 ppm	1.2% or 12,000 ppm	7.8% or 78,000 ppm
Ethyl Benzene	100 ppm	800 ppm	0.8% or 8000 ppm	6.7% or 67,000 ppm
Toluene	200 ppm	500 ppm	1.1% or 11,000 ppm	7.1% or 71,000 ppm
Xylenes	100 ppm	900 ppm	0.9% or 9000 ppm	7% or 70,000 ppm
n-Hexane	500 ppm	1100 ppm	1.1% or 11,000 ppm	7.5% or 75,000 ppm
Mixed petroleum hydrocarbons (Naphthas, aliphatic and aromatic compounds)	500 ppm	1100 ppm	1.1% or 11,000 ppm	5.9% or 59,000 ppm

*Source OSHA Permissible Exposure Limits – Annotated Tables Z-1 and Z-2.

** Source NFPA 325 "Guide to Fire Hazard Properties of Flammable Liquids, Gases and Volatile Solids, 1994 edition and NIOSH Pocket Guide to Chemical Hazards, 2005-2010 DHHS (NIOSH) Publication No. 2010-168c CD-ROM.

Note that while the OSHA PELs must be followed, NFPA 325 and the NIOSH Pocket Guide to Chemical Hazards provide additional guidance information on the listed chemicals.

Section VI – Employer Responsibility to Protect Workers

Under the *Occupational Safety and Health Act of 1970*, employers are responsible for providing safe and healthful working conditions for their workers.

Worker Rights

Workers have the right to:

- Working conditions that do not pose a risk of serious harm.

- Receive information and training (in a language and vocabulary the worker understands) about workplace hazards, methods to prevent them, and the OSHA standards that apply to their workplace.

- Review records of work-related injuries and illnesses.

- File a complaint asking OSHA to inspect their workplace if they believe there is a serious hazard or that their employer is not following OSHA's rules. OSHA will keep all identities confidential.

- Exercise their rights under the law without retaliation, including reporting an injury or raising health and safety concerns with their employer or OSHA. If a worker has been retaliated against for using their rights, they must file a complaint with OSHA as soon as possible, but no later than 30 days.

For more information, see OSHA's Workers page.

OSHA Assistance, Services and Programs

OSHA has a great deal of information to assist employers in complying with their responsibilities under OSHA law. Several OSHA programs and services can help employers identify and correct job hazards, as well as improve their injury and illness prevention program.

Establishing an Injury and Illness Prevention Program

The key to a safe and healthful work environment is a comprehensive injury and illness prevention program.

Injury and illness prevention programs are systems that can substantially reduce the number and severity of workplace injuries and illnesses, while reducing costs to employers. Thousands of employers across the United States already manage safety using injury and illness prevention programs, and OSHA believes that all employers can and should do the same. Thirty-four states have requirements or voluntary guidelines for workplace injury and illness prevention programs. Most successful injury and illness prevention programs are based on a common set of key elements. These include management leadership, worker participation, hazard identification, hazard prevention and control, education and training, and program evaluation and improvement. Visit OSHA's Injury and Illness Prevention Programs web page at www.osha.gov/dsg/topics/safetyhealth for more information.

Compliance Assistance Specialists

OSHA has compliance assistance specialists throughout the nation located in most OSHA offices. Compliance assistance specialists can provide information to employers and workers about OSHA standards, short educational programs on specific hazards or OSHA rights and responsibilities, and information on additional compliance assistance resources. For more details, visit www.osha.gov/dcsp/compliance_assistance/cas.html or call 1-800-321-OSHA (6742) to contact your local OSHA office.

Free On-site Safety and Health Consultation Services for Small Business

OSHA's On-site Consultation Program offers free and confidential advice to small and medium-sized businesses in all states across the country, with priority given to high-hazard worksites. Each year, responding to requests from small employers looking to create or improve their safety and health management programs, OSHA's On-site Consultation Program conducts over 29,000 visits to small business worksites covering over 1.5 million workers across the nation.

On-site consultation services are separate from enforcement and do not result in penalties or citations. Consultants from state agencies or universities work with employers to identify workplace hazards, provide advice on compliance with OSHA standards, and assist in establishing safety and health management programs.

For more information, to find the local On-site Consultation office in your state, or to request a brochure on Consultation Services, visit www.osha.gov/consultation, or call 1-800-321-OSHA (6742).

Under the consultation program, certain exemplary employers may request participation in OSHA's **Safety and Health Achievement Recognition Program (SHARP)**. Eligibility for participation includes, but is not limited to, receiving a full-service, comprehensive consultation visit, correcting all identified hazards and developing an effective safety and health management program. Worksites that receive SHARP recognition are exempt from programmed inspections during the period that the SHARP certification is valid.

Cooperative Programs

OSHA offers cooperative programs under which businesses, labor groups and other organizations can work cooperatively with OSHA. To find out more about any of the following programs, visit www.osha.gov/cooperativeprograms.

Strategic Partnerships and Alliances

The OSHA Strategic Partnerships (OSP) provide the opportunity for OSHA to partner with employers, workers, professional or trade associations, labor organizations, and/or other interested stakeholders. OSHA Partnerships are formalized through unique agreements designed to encourage, assist, and recognize partner efforts to eliminate serious hazards and achieve model workplace safety and health practices. Through the Alliance Program, OSHA works with groups committed to worker safety and health to prevent workplace fatalities, injuries and illnesses by developing compliance assistance tools and resources to share with workers and employers, and educate workers and employers about their rights and responsibilities.

Voluntary Protection Programs (VPP)

The VPP recognize employers and workers in private industry and federal agencies who have implemented effective safety and health management programs and maintain injury and illness rates below the national average for their respective industries. In VPP, management, labor, and OSHA work cooperatively and proactively to prevent fatalities, injuries, and illnesses through a system focused on: hazard prevention and control, worksite analysis, training, and management commitment and worker involvement.

Occupational Safety and Health Training

The OSHA Training Institute in Arlington Heights, Illinois, provides basic and advanced training and education in safety and health for federal and state compliance officers, state consultants, other federal agency personnel and private sector employers, workers, and their representatives. In addition, 27 OSHA Training Institute Education Centers at 42 locations throughout the United States deliver courses on OSHA standards and occupational safety and health issues to thousands of students a year.

For more information on training, contact the OSHA Directorate of Training and Education, 2020 Arlington Heights Road, Arlington Heights, IL 60005; call 1-847-297-4810; or visit www.osha.gov/otiec.

OSHA Educational Materials

OSHA has many types of educational materials in English, Spanish, Vietnamese and other languages available in print or online. These include:

- Brochures/booklets that cover a wide variety of job hazards and other topics;

- Fact Sheets, which contain basic background information on safety and health hazards;

- Guidance documents that provide detailed examinations of specific safety and health issues;

- Online Safety and Health Topics pages;

- Posters;

- Small, laminated QuickCards™ that provide brief safety and health information; and

- *QuickTakes*, OSHA's free, twice-monthly online newsletter with the latest news about OSHA initiatives and products to assist employers and workers in finding and preventing workplace hazards. To sign up for *QuickTakes* visit www.osha.gov/quicktakes.

To view materials available online or for a listing of free publications, visit www.osha.gov/publications. You can also call 1-800-321-OSHA (6742) to order publications.

OSHA's web site also has a variety of eTools. These include utilities such as expert advisors, electronic compliance assistance, videos and other information for employers and workers. To learn more about OSHA's safety and health tools online, visit www.osha.gov.

NIOSH Health Hazard Evaluation Program

Getting Help with Health Hazards

The National Institute for Occupational Safety and Health (NIOSH) is a federal agency that conducts scientific and medical research on workers' safety and health. At no cost to employers or workers, NIOSH can help identify health hazards and recommend ways to reduce or eliminate those hazards in the workplace through its Health Hazard Evaluation (HHE) Program.

Workers, union representatives and employers can request a NIOSH HHE. An HHE is often requested when there is a higher than expected rate of a disease or injury in a group of workers. These situations may be the result of an unknown cause, a new hazard, or a mixture of sources. To request a NIOSH Health Hazard Evaluation go to www.cdc.gov/niosh/hhe/request.html. To find out more about the Health Hazard Evaluation Program:

- Call (513) 841-4382, or to talk to a staff member in Spanish, call (513) 841-4439; or
- Send an email to HHERequestHelp@cdc.gov.

OSHA Regional Offices

Region I
Boston Regional Office
(CT*, ME, MA, NH, RI, VT*)
JFK Federal Building, Room E340
Boston, MA 02203
(617) 565-9860 (617) 565-9827 Fax

Region II
New York Regional Office
(NJ*, NY*, PR*, VI*)
201 Varick Street, Room 670
New York, NY 10014
(212) 337-2378 (212) 337-2371 Fax

Region III
Philadelphia Regional Office
(DE, DC, MD*, PA, VA*, WV)
The Curtis Center
170 S. Independence Mall West
Suite 740 West
Philadelphia, PA 19106-3309
(215) 861-4900 (215) 861-4904 Fax

Region IV
Atlanta Regional Office
(AL, FL, GA, KY*, MS, NC*, SC*, TN*)
61 Forsyth Street, SW, Room 6T50
Atlanta, GA 30303
(678) 237-0400 (678) 237-0447 Fax

Region V
Chicago Regional Office
(IL*, IN*, MI*, MN*, OH, WI)
230 South Dearborn Street
Room 3244
Chicago, IL 60604
(312) 353-2220 (312) 353-7774 Fax

Region VI
Dallas Regional Office
(AR, LA, NM*, OK, TX)
525 Griffin Street, Room 602
Dallas, TX 75202
(972) 850-4145 (972) 850-4149 Fax
(972) 850-4150 FSO Fax

Region VII
Kansas City Regional Office
(IA*, KS, MO, NE)
Two Pershing Square Building
2300 Main Street, Suite 1010
Kansas City, MO 64108-2416
(816) 283-8745 (816) 283-0547 Fax

Region VIII
Denver Regional Office
(CO, MT, ND, SD, UT*, WY*)
Cesar Chavez Memorial Building
1244 Speer Boulevard, Suite 551
Denver, CO 80204
(720) 264-6550 (720) 264-6585 Fax

Region IX
San Francisco Regional Office
(AZ*, CA*, HI*, NV*, and American Samoa,
Guam and the Northern Mariana Islands)
90 7th Street, Suite 18100
San Francisco, CA 94103
(415) 625-2547 (415) 625-2534 Fax

Region X
Seattle Regional Office
(AK*, ID, OR*, WA*)
300 Fifth Avenue, Suite 1280
Seattle, WA 98104
(206) 757-6700 (206) 757-6705 Fax

* These states and territories operate
their own OSHA-approved job safety and
health plans and cover state and local
government employees as well as private

sector employees. The Connecticut, Illinois, New Jersey, New York and Virgin Islands programs cover public employees only. (Private sector workers in these states are covered by Federal OSHA). States with approved programs must have standards that are identical to, or at least as effective as, the Federal OSHA standards.

Note: To get contact information for OSHA area offices, OSHA-approved state plans and OSHA consultation projects, please visit us online at www.osha.gov or call us at 1-800-321-OSHA (6742).

How to Contact OSHA

For questions or to get information or advice, to report an emergency, report a fatality or catastrophe, order publications, sign up for OSHA's e-newsletter *QuickTakes*, or to file a confidential complaint, contact your nearest OSHA office, visit www.osha.gov or call OSHA at 1-800-321-OSHA (6742), TTY 1-877-889-5627.

Appendix A – Flow Chart of Processes

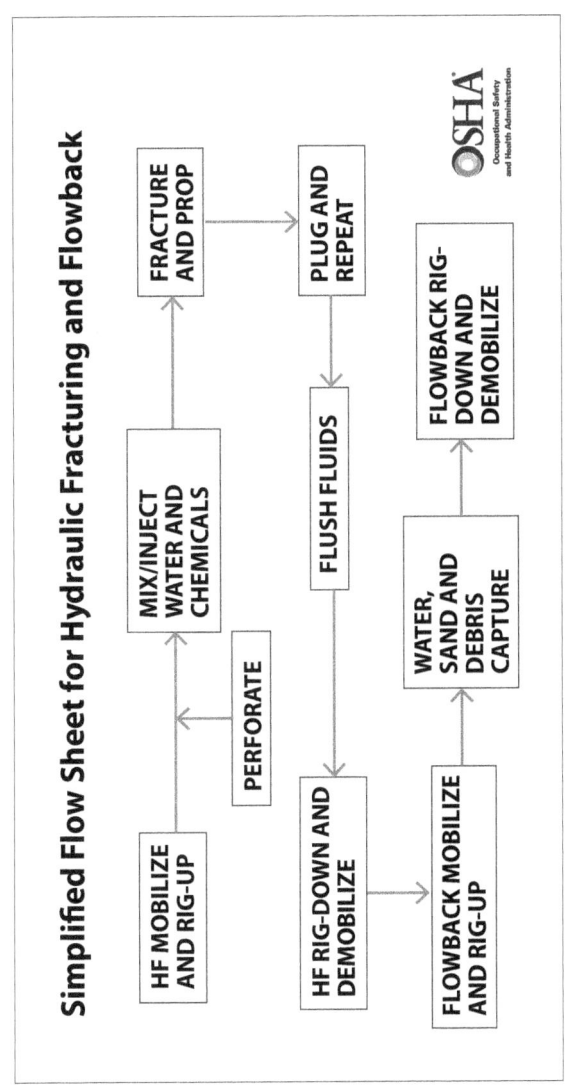

Simplified Flow Sheet for Hydraulic Fracturing and Flowback

HF MOBILIZE AND RIG-UP → PERFORATE → MIX/INJECT WATER AND CHEMICALS → FRACTURE AND PROP → PLUG AND REPEAT → FLUSH FLUIDS → HF RIG-DOWN AND DEMOBILIZE → FLOWBACK MOBILIZE AND RIG-UP → WATER, SAND AND DEBRIS CAPTURE → FLOWBACK RIG-DOWN AND DEMOBILIZE

OSHA
Occupational Safety and Health Administration

Appendix B – Oil Patch Fatality Rate

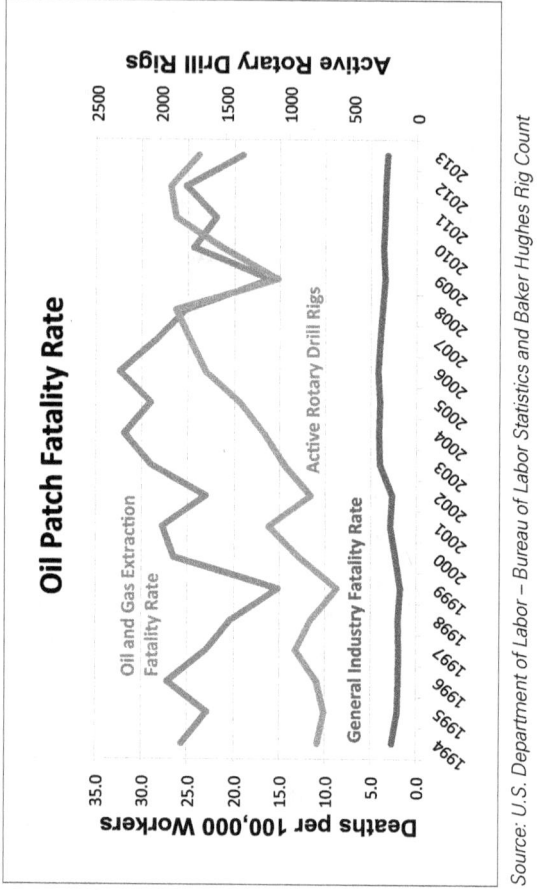

Source: U.S. Department of Labor – Bureau of Labor Statistics and Baker Hughes Rig Count

Appendix C – Links to Additional Resources

The resources identified below supplement the information provided in each of the corresponding sections of this document.

Introduction

- Oil and Gas Well Drilling, Servicing and Storage Safety and Health Topics Page
- Oil and Gas Well Drilling and Servicing eTool

Section I

- Motor Vehicle Safety
- Motor Vehicle Safety – Construction
- Distracted Driving
- Motor Vehicle Fact Sheet
- Ergonomics Safety and Health Topics Page

Section II

- Hazard Communication Publication
- Hazard Communication Safety and Health Topics Page

Section IV

- Fire Safety Fact Sheet

Section V

- The H_2S Safety and Health Topics Page
- The H_2S Fact Sheet
- Fire Safety Fact Sheet

Appendix D – Potential Hazards Related Hydraulic Fracturing

Job Steps in Well Stimulation	Potentially Affected Crews/ Personnel	Traffic Control	Journey Mgt.	Simops	Lifting / Rigging	Unplanned Release of Stored Energy	Chemical Exposure	Crystalline Silica	Diesel Exhaust	Other Atmospheric Hazards/H_2S	Flammable Atmosphere	Struck By (e.g., Line Whipping)	Caught Between	Fall from Elevation
Travel to Site	Hydraulic Fracturing (HF), Rigging, Tank Haulers (Water, Chemicals, Acids), Wire Line, Rental Equipment/Heavy Equipment Movers, Flowback, liners, matters, cranes, water transfer and sand haulers	X	X						X					
Pre-stimulation site prep	Set Liner, mats set, set frac tanks, sand masters, water lines, HCL tank rig-up	X		X	X	X			X			X	X	X
Stimulation Rig-up	HF Rigging, Haulers (Water, Chemicals, Proppant), Wire Line, Rental Equipment/Heavy Equipment Movers, crane set-up	X	X	X	X	X	X	X	X			X	X	X
Set Piping/ Manifolding	HF, pull tubing, wire line, water transfer, flowback, chemical transfer, testing rigs			X	X	X	X					X	X	X
Chemical and Acid RigUp/ Blending	Tank Haulers, blender, chemical company, pumpers			X	X	X	X	X	X	X	X	X	X	X
Set Lubricator	Wire line crew, HF operation, coil tubing, crane			X	X				X			X	X	X
Pressure Test	Flowback, water transfer, chemical transfer, pump trucks, coil tubing/ rig, testing rigs			X	X	X	X		X			X		
Perforating, Plugging	Wire Line, gun technician, coil tubing, rig, HF crews, chemical crew			X	X	X	X		X		X	X	X	X
Fuel Handling	Fuel Company, pump trucks	X	X	X		X	X	X	X	X	X	X	X	
Proppant Transport/ Handling	Truck Haulers, Blenders, HF Crew	X	X	X		X	X	X	X			X	X	X
Pumping/ Setting Plugs	HF Crew and Fluid Samplers, wire lines, coil tubing, blending /Acidizing, Chemical Crew,			X	X	X	X	X	X			X	X	X

to the Job Steps of

Slips, Trips and Falls	Confined Space	Dropped Objects	Power Lines	Stray Voltage	Mismatched Components	Lose Control of Lift	Working under Suspended Load	Unplanned Detonation	Fire and Explosion	Radio Transmission	Control System Failure	Equipment Failure	Unplanned Spill or Physical Contact	Radiation Exposure	Erosion Failure/Leak	Thermal	Energy Isolation	Pressure Control
		X									X	X						
X	X	X	X		X	X	X				X	X						
X	X	X				X					X				X			
X	X				X	X	X				X	X	X	X	X	X		X
X	X				X	X	X	X	X		X	X	X		X	X	X	X
X	X	X				X	X				X	X						
X						X					X	X			X	X	X	X
X	X	X			X	X	X	X	X	X	X	X	X				X	X
X		X	X						X		X	X	X				X	X
X											X	X	X					
X		X	X						X		X	X	X	X	X	X	X	X

Hydraulic Fracturing Potential Hazards and Job Steps		Traffic Control	Journey Mgt.	Simops	Lifting / Rigging	Unplanned Release of Stored Energy	Chemical Exposure	Crystalline Silica	Diesel Exhaust	Other Atmospheric Hazards/H_2S	Flammable Atmosphere	Struck By (e.g., Line Whipping)	Caught Between	Fall from Elevation	Slips, Trips and Falls
Job Steps in Well Stimulation	Potentially Affected Crews/ Personnel														
Rig Down Stimulation	HF Rigging, Haulers (Water, Chemicals, Proppant), Wire Line, Rental Equipment/Heavy Equipment Movers, crane set-up	X	X	X	X	X	X	X	X			X	X	X	X
Rig Up Flowback	Flowback Crew, Coil Tubing/Rig Crew, Crane Crew, H_2S Safety Crew, Line Restraint, Anchor / Pull Test Crew,	X	X	X	X	X	X	X	X			X	X	X	X
Flowback	Flowback Crew, Coil Tubing/Rig Crew, Crane Crew, H_2S Safety Crew, Oil and Water Haulers, Water Transfer	X		X		X	X			X	X	X	X	X	X
Rig Down/ Flowback	Flowback Crew, Coil Tubing/Rig Crew, Crane Crew, H_2S Safety Crew, Line Restraint Crew, Trucking Crew, Water Transfer	X	X	X	X	X	X	X	X			X	X	X	X

Hazard	1	2	3	4
Confined Space		X		
Dropped Objects	X	X		X
Power Lines	X	X		X
Stray Voltage			X	
Mismatched Components			X	
Lose Control of Lift	X	X		X
Working under Suspended Load	X	X		X
Unplanned Detonation		X		
Fire and Explosion			X	
Radio Transmission				
Control System Failure			X	
Equipment Failure	X	X	X	X
Unplanned Spill or Physical Contact		X	X	X
Radiation Exposure			X	X
Erosion Failure/Leak			X	
Thermal	X			
Energy Isolation	X			
Pressure Control			X	

**For assistance, contact us.
We are OSHA. We can help.**